or Ajax and Hopper and the Hooded Claw —J.P.L

old friend, and my new friend, Allan Markman

For Megan, Paxton, and Charlie —J.H.

"[Introductory Car Poem]," "Giant Bookmobile of Tomorrow," "Eel-ectric Car,"
"Jurassic Park(ing)," "High-Heel Car," "23rd-Century Motors," "Balloon Car," "Bathtub
Car," "Grass Taxi," and "The Banana Split Car" copyright © 2014 by J. Patrick Lewis

"Mini-Mini-Car," "Fish Car," "The Dragonwagon," "The Paper Car," "The Backwards Car,"
"Caterpillar Cab," "The Egg Car," "Hot Dog Car," "The Sloppy-Floppy-Nonstop-Jalopy,"
"The Love Car," "The Supersonic Ionic Car," and "Rubber-Band Car"
copyright © 2014 by Douglas Florian

Illustrations copyright © 2014 by Jeremy Holmes

Educators and librarians, for a variety of teaching tools,
visit us at RHTeachersLibrarians.com

Library of Congress Cataloging-in-Publication Data
Lewis, J. Patrick.
Poem-Mobiles: Crazy Car Poems / J. Patrick Lewis and Douglas Florian ;
illustrated by Jeremy Holmes.—1st ed.
p. cm.
ISBN 978-0-375-86690-6 (trade) —ISBN 978-0-375-96690-3 (glb)
ISBN 978-0-375-98764-9 (ebook)
1. Automobiles—Poetry. 2. Children's poetry, American. I. Florian, Douglas.
II. Holmes, Jeremy, ill. III. Title.
PS3562.E9465B44 2011
811'.54—dc22
2011011023

The text of this book is set in Swiss Piccola.
The illustrations were rendered in pencil and watercolor, then digitally colored.

MANUFACTURED IN CHINA
10 8 6 4 2 1 3 5 7 9
First Edition

POEM-MOBILES

CRAZY CAR POEMS

J. PATRICK LEWIS and DOUGLAS FLORIAN

pictures by JEREMY HOLMES

* * *

schwartz & wade books · new york

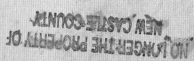

CONTENTS

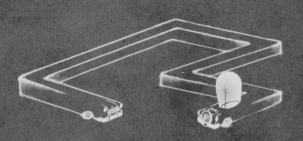

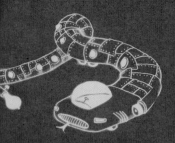
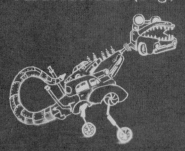

Introduction

* * *

<u>Train</u> means <u>train</u>, <u>bus</u> means <u>bus</u>,
<u>Truck</u> means <u>truck</u> to most of us.

So <u>auto</u> ought to mean, you see,
<u>Auto</u> automatically.

But someday our fantastic cars
Might look like cool dark chocolate bars,

Banana splits, hot dogs or fish—
Or any kind of ride you wish.

And so we'd like to offer you
A futuristic sneak preview

Of wacky cars, fender to fin.
Now turn the page and take a spin.

Giant Bookmobile of Tomorrow

* * *

I am a <u>very</u> moving van.
Driver: he's the Gingerbread Man.
Fuel: imagination power.
Speed: a dozen aisles per hour.
Whether it be comic strips,
Poetry at your fingertips,
Picture books or trivia,
<u>The</u> <u>Wizard</u> <u>of</u> <u>Oz</u>, <u>Olivia</u>,
My bookmobile has just one goal:
To entertain on cruise control.
But kids get on at every block
And I forget to watch the clock.
So if my van is "overdue,"
It's okay if you are too.

Mini-Mini-Car

* * *

I'm in my little motorcar—
My mini-mini-mini.
It's itsy-bitsy-teeny-weeny,
Skinny skinny skinny.
I squeeze inside and then I ride
Some more and more and more.
But I don't brag, for there's a snag:
I can't get out the door.

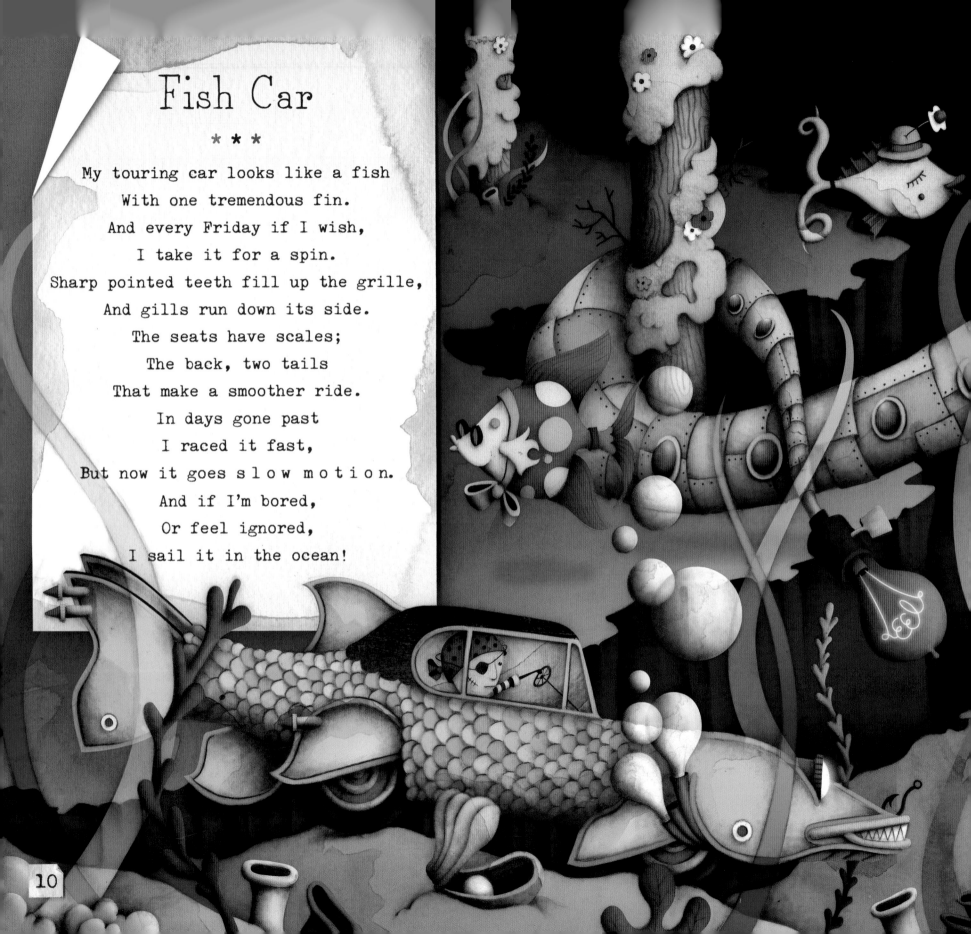

Fish Car

* * *

My touring car looks like a fish
With one tremendous fin.
And every Friday if I wish,
I take it for a spin.
Sharp pointed teeth fill up the grille,
And gills run down its side.
The seats have scales;
The back, two tails
That make a smoother ride.
In days gone past
I raced it fast,
But now it goes s l o w   m o t i o n.
And if I'm bored,
Or feel ignored,
I sail it in the ocean!

Eel-ectric Car

* * *

By day I curve around the pier,
at night I swerve . . .
Bring scuba gear!
Hang on until you get the feel
of my eel-ectric steering wheel.
My spark plugs spark—
now watch me peel!
I'm a battery-powered
a u t o m o b EEEEEEEEEL!

Jurassic Park(ing)

* * *

You thought the dinosaurs were dead?!
The cars behind our school
Are big Tyrannosaurus wrecks
That run on fossil fuel.

The Dragonwagon

* * *

The Dragonwagon's painted green:
A scary, scaly mean machine.
Its wings are capable of flying
Above all traffic that comes by.
Upon its back are nasty spikes.
It feeds with greed on rusty bikes.
Inside its hood are toothy jaws.
Instead of wheels, it has sharp claws
That hug the road and sharply turn.
Its fiery breath is built to burn
All creatures coming in its path—
Don't dare provoke this dragon's wrath!

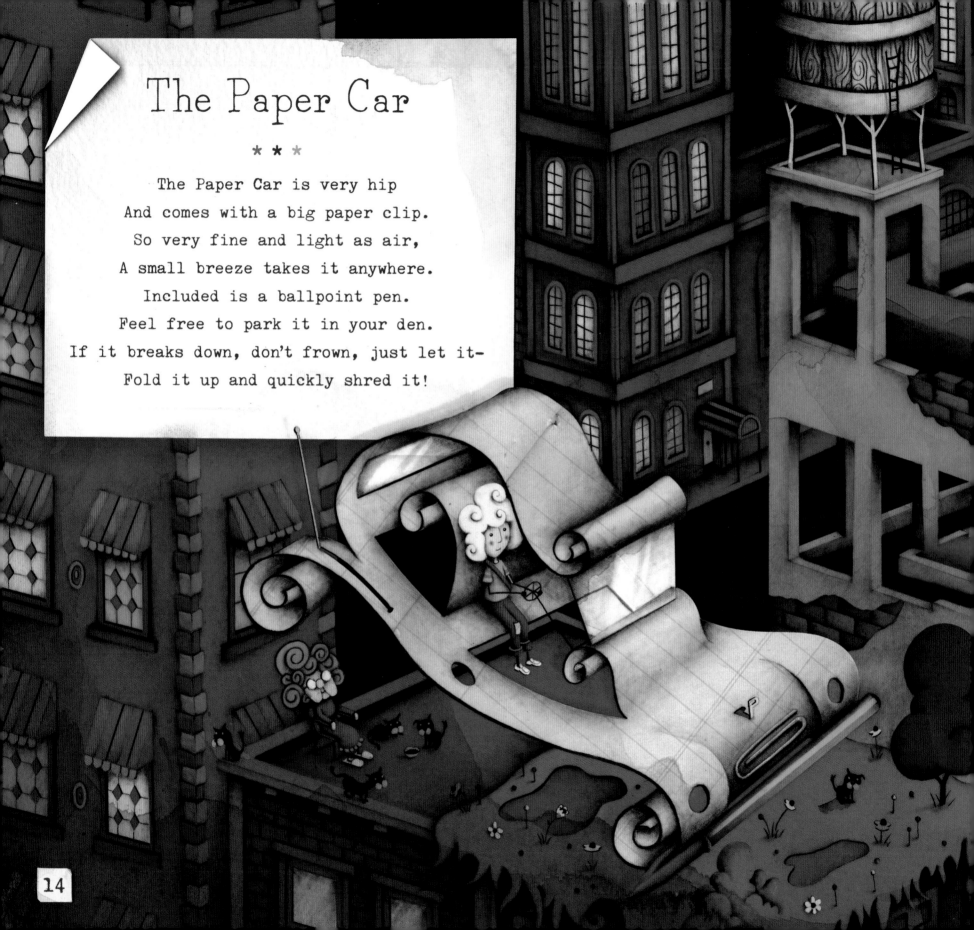

The Paper Car

* * *

The Paper Car is very hip
And comes with a big paper clip.
So very fine and light as air,
A small breeze takes it anywhere.
Included is a ballpoint pen.
Feel free to park it in your den.
If it breaks down, don't frown, just let it—
Fold it up and quickly shred it!

The Backwards Car

* * *

The Backwards Car
Goes in reverse
Both near and far.
And what is worse,
The things you've seen
Are not ahead,
But where you've been
Thus far instead.
Instead of going
To
And
Fro,
From fro
To
To
You likely go.
And when you're there
And you arrive,
You find you're where
You launched your drive.

15

High-Heel Car

***

There was an old woman
Who lived in high heels.
She loved one so much
That she gave it three wheels.

That's how the size-84
Shoe-car was born!
She wins every footrace,
Then honks her shoehorn.

16

23rd-Century Motors

* * *

Here's what we will be driving
When oil and gasoline
Are just a distant memory—
The family li-mooo-sine.

Balloon Car

* * *

My daddy drives a car that floats
an inch above the street—
a hundred colorful balloons
tied to a bucket seat.

And once he blows his car up,
Daddy never wants to stop.
But boy, does he get mad at me
When I call out—"Hey, POP!"

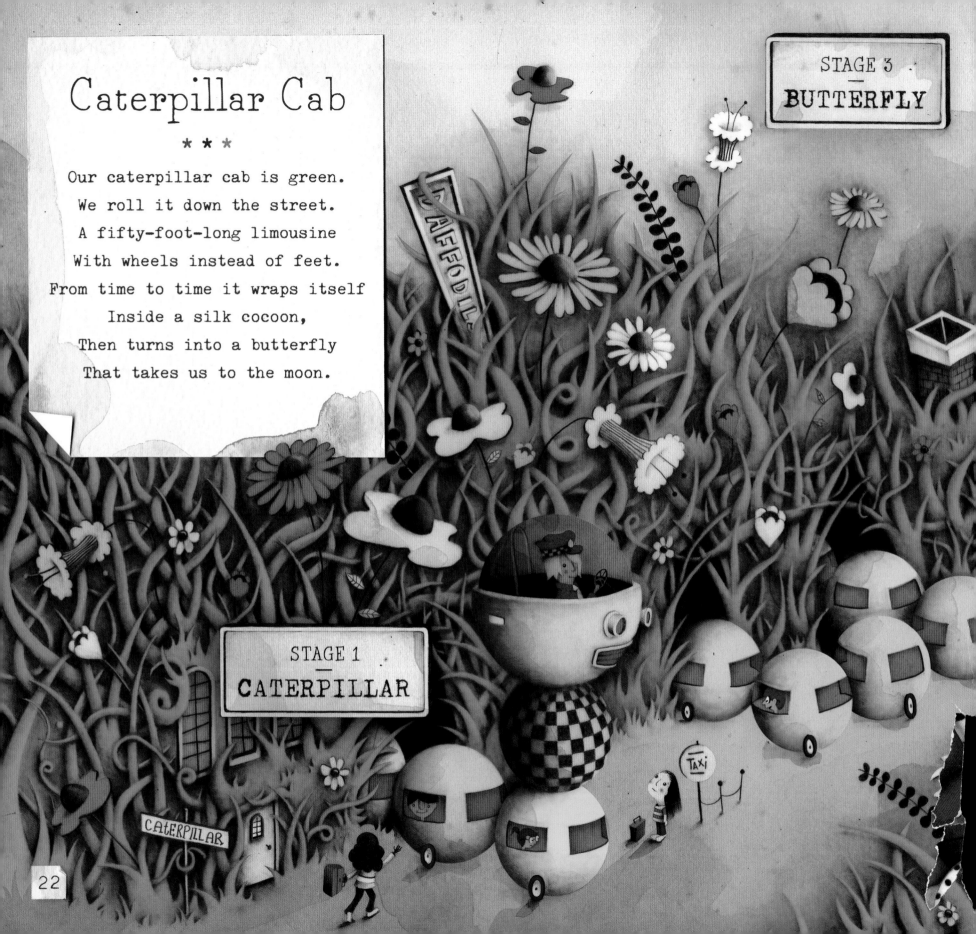

Caterpillar Cab

* * *

Our caterpillar cab is green.
We roll it down the street.
A fifty-foot-long limousine
With wheels instead of feet.
From time to time it wraps itself
Inside a silk cocoon,
Then turns into a butterfly
That takes us to the moon.

STAGE 3
—
BUTTERFLY

STAGE 1
—
CATERPILLAR

Bathtub Car

* * *

With hot-water heating
And porcelain seating,
The Bathtub is speeding—
A white limousine

That's sudsy with bubbles.
Forget your car troubles.
Its purpose? It doubles
By keeping you clean!

ROYAL THRONE

25

The Egg Car

* * *

The egg car doesn't need a wheel—
You roll it down the street.
Just plop on top from stop to stop
And steer it with your feet.
Make no mistake: there is no brake—
You slow down with your legs.
Or else you'll crash, most likely smash,
And sit in scrambled eggs.

Hot Dog Car

* * *

My hot dog car is lots of fun
And comes with relish on a bun.
It runs on tons of sauerkraut
Or mustard when you've just run out.
Enjoy its fine and fragrant smell.
Its color has no parallel.
My hot dog car—
You just can't beat it.
And when you're done
You simply eat it.

The Sloppy-Floppy-Nonstop-Jalopy

* * *

The Sloppy-Floppy-Nonstop-Jalopy
Is so unique—there is no copy.
The horn's a big brass slide trombone.
The steering wheel's a telephone.
The roof is made from bark of birch,
On top of which six seagulls perch.
The engine's crafted from tin cans,
A coffeepot and frying pans.
Each seat's a throne from Zanzibar
Complete with eat-in salad bar.
The tires are all fashioned from
Some slightly used pink bubble gum.
The radio can get the news
From any planet you may choose.
The wheels are from the Colosseum.
It's not a car—
It's a museum!

Grass Taxi

* * *

I need to mow the glass,
I should Weedwack the visor,
I'm blanketed in grass.
My wax is fertilizer.
And when my gas tank's low,
I fill up on Weed-B-Gone.
My wormy engine's slow.
Check underneath my lawn.

29

The Love Car

* * *

I ♡ the shape.

I ♡ the hue.

I ♡ to drive my love car too.

I ♡ the shine.

I ♡ the wheels.

I ♡ the way my love car feels.

I ♡ the seats.

I ♡ the lights.

I ♡ my love car

Day and night.

31

The Banana Split Car

* * *

That's not brown paint,
It's chocolate fudge.
And here and there,
A whipped-cream smudge.
The light on top's
A real cherry!
They sell this car
At Motor Dairy—
This Model T(spoon's)
One sweet deal.
Besides, it's got
Bananappeal!

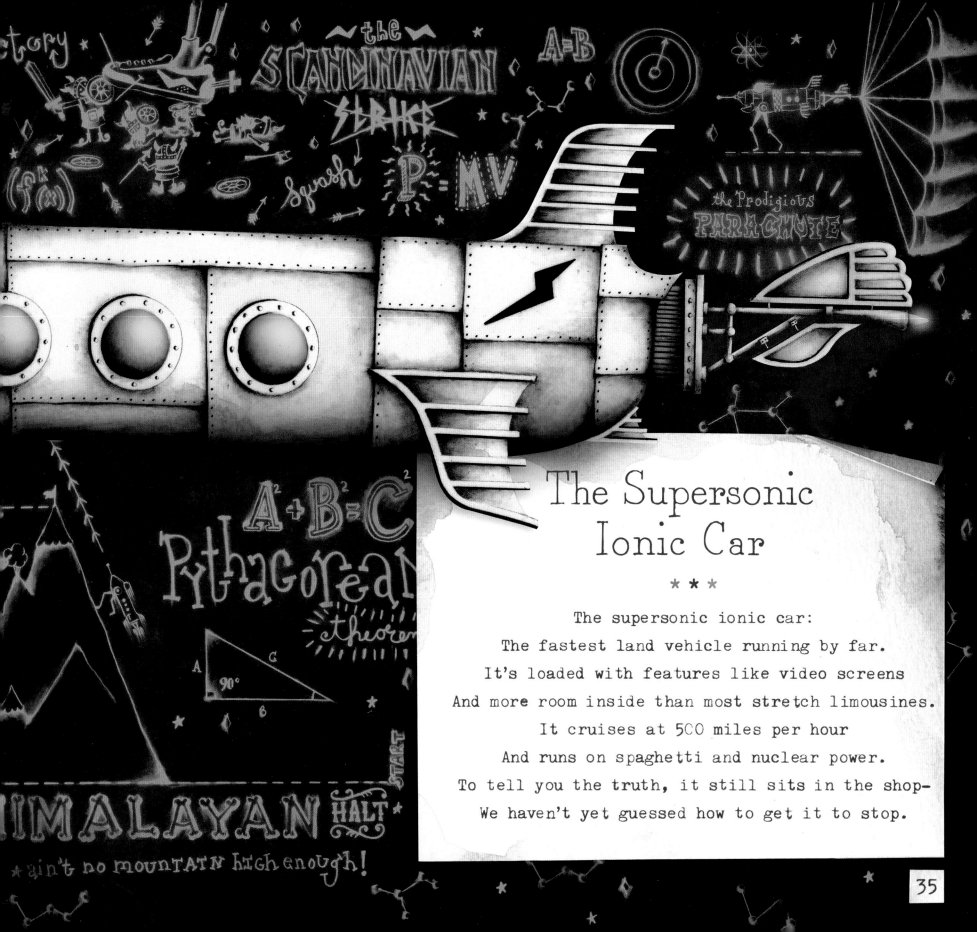

The Supersonic Ionic Car

* * *

The supersonic ionic car:
The fastest land vehicle running by far.
It's loaded with features like video screens
And more room inside than most stretch limousines.
It cruises at 500 miles per hour
And runs on spaghetti and nuclear power.
To tell you the truth, it still sits in the shop—
We haven't yet guessed how to get it to stop.

Rubber-Band Car

* * *

Bouncing, bounding down the road
Like a leaping, beeping toad.
Made from giant rubber bands
(Very pliant in your hands).
It jumps over traffic jams,
And obstructions gently rams.
It can float just like a barge,
Takes three spots in a garage.
Needs no shocks and needs no springs.
And to fly it, just add wings.
Outperforms all other cars—
One bounced all the way to Mars.

The End